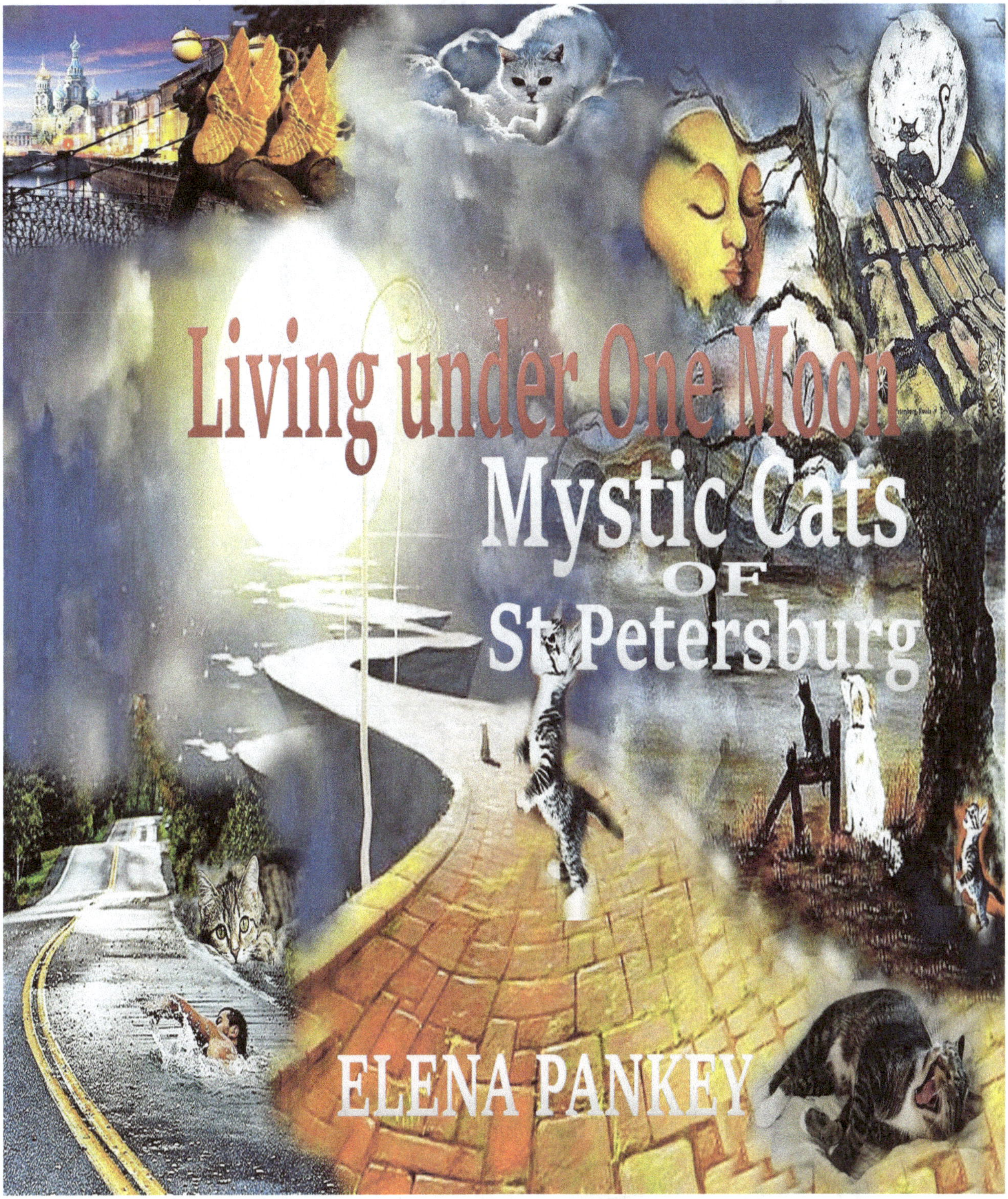
Living under One Moon
Mystic Cats
OF
St.Petersburg
ELENA PANKEY

ISBN: 978-1-950311-82-8

978-1-950311-82-8

I0380143

Living under One Moon

Mystic Cats of St. Petersburg

Elena Pankey

ISBN: 978-1-950311-82-8

AllRightsReserved@2020ElenaPankey

No copyright infringement is intended

Contents

About book	3
Kittens	4
Magical St. Petersburg	5
Sphinx	7
Legend	9
Griffins	12
Walks	16
Promenade	18
PART TWO	20
Good girl Lila	22
New home	23
Cleanliness	24
New rules	26
Cat Revenge	27
New Year	28
March cats	34
Cat 's Flights	35
Help	37
Train	40
Arrival	42
Unexpected	47
Tosha's Victory	48
Feline art	50
Next nights	51
Returned	51
PART THREE	53
Solution	56
Puppy	56
Tosha and Break	58
	59

Respect	63
Games	65
Winter	67
Tosha's Hobby	69
Be useful	70
Family vacation	71
Vacation	72
Dog School	73
Circumstances	75
Tosha's Dream	77
One Moon to Love	78
Our pets	78
About the author	80

Cat Murka, cat Vasily and their friends are in of St. Petersburg

***

About book

This fascinating and colorful book is for children. It contain many photos, drawings and funny stories of the Author's real cat Tosha and her dog Break. It has instructive facts from the life of cats.

The first part is about the magic city of Russia - St. Petersburg. It gives the short information about the embankments of the city, where cats live and have fun. There is a story about the birth of kitten Tosha, about his friends who lived under the bridges of a magical city on the Neva River. Cats strive to be similar to their distant relatives – lions. Many sculptures of lions are everywhere on the embankments. Cat Vasily told legends of the sphinx and griffins.

The second part is about Tosha's flights from the balcony, his trip to the Black Sea, his nightly adventures and battles with the local cats on the Black sea. Tosha was sure that he was the highest being, and sought to subjugate all who lived nearby. When he happened to visit Gelendzik, he met local cats there and fought for his life. Then, cat Tosha reevaluated his St. Petersburg sybaritic life. He began to cherish everything that he had before his trip to the South.

The third part is about the friendship of the cat Tosha with a puppy named Brake.

Entertaining information about the character and habits of our beloved pets will allow parents to share a pleasant time with their children while reading these books. Joint pastime will make life much more joyful.

***

Kittens

Once upon a time, and maybe even now, in the beautiful, northern city of Russia there were cats and cats. Although it rained often in the city, the magical city often shone with amazing colors. And it was built more than three hundred years ago on the banks of the wide Neva River. It was called St. Petersburg, or the city of St. Peter. The city has long been the northern capital of Russia.

Once under the Palace Bridge of that magical city of St. Petersburg, cat Murka had a lot of new tiny kittens. Kittens were born in the warm, wonderful summer day. At that time different fast boats sailed along the Neva River. The kittens had many relatives who lived right there nearby. They all came to visit cat Murka and congratulate her with new children.

Mommy Murka was proud of her work and full of love for her children. Several times a day she carefully licked them all. The first few days the kitten's eyes were not open. They only sucked mother's milk and slept. When it was the time for their feeding, the cat Murka comfortably laid on a fluffy rug. Kittens crawled and snuggled up close to her belly. Murka smiled blissfully and purred: "Oh, you are my little ones! Oh, my dear ones."

Usually, all kittens have born blue-eyed. But gradually, by the age of three months, the color of the eyes of the kittens began to change. Then, after a while, they all quickly grew up. Almost all her kittens were very smart. Some others were a little bit mischievous. But mommy Murka hoped that when they grow up, they will receive an excellent education, and will be happy and successful. In the meantime, the cat Murka comfortably lay next to her children, and guarded them from everyone, including predatory gulls.

Also, dad Vasily and mommy Murka loved each other very much, as well. On weekends, they sometimes even went to the Moika River. And there, hugging comfortably, they usually rest after a long walk. At that time, their eldest son did not like to sit with no job. He immediately pulled out his fishing rods and started fishing. He also periodically was watching the new kittens, who squeak in a large box.

So, the kittens were born under the Palace Bridge, in a magical city of St. Petersburg.

That magical city had many palaces, many bridges and sculptures. Mommy Murka hoped that such beautiful environment would develop in her children good taste and style. So, when children grew a little bit more, cat Vasily and mommy Murka began to take them on a long walks.

During the walks cats talked about different amazing monuments and wonders of the city, where they lived.

Magical St. Petersburg

Mommy Murka told her children that the magnificent embankments and bridges were gradually built along the Neva River. In the summer, the sun goes to sleep only for a short time. Therefore, the nights in the city are bright, and they are called "White Nights". During the "White Nights" huge bridges are opened over the wide Neva. The tall ships go under the bridges towards the Baltic Sea to other countries. That is why the city and was called "window to the Europe."

At different times, many sculptures of animals, birds, lions, horses, eagles were installed in it to decorate the city. Especially a lot of sphinxes and lions were there made of different materials. They brought from China, Israel, Italy and some of them created in Russia.

The lion is the king of animals. Therefore he is a symbol of courage, strength, power and greatness. In ancient time, it was believed that lions sleep with their eyes open. People thought, they are ideal guardians, protecting a house or city from some evil spirits. Lion statues were installed at the entrance to temples and palaces.

The Great Russian Tsar Peter I, soon after the founding of St. Petersburg, decided to make the city the capital of a powerful Russian empire. He dreamed that his city would become as magnificent as Ancient Rome. Therefore, lions were appropriate in the city.

Many guardian lions in the city keep their paws on the ball so they don't fall asleep. The tale says that if the lion falls asleep, then his paw will slide off the ball. The lion will wake up and be angry, but still continue to guard the city.

Under bridges and on the embankments of this magical city cats live. They think that they are the distant relatives of lions. The big family of cat Murka and cat Vasily lives there, as well. During the White Nights, cats play and rest on the embankments. They could see the sculptures of Lions near the river. These Lions are also called philosophers and thinkers, because they are very serious and thoughtful.

In St. Petersburg, there are a lot of monuments of lions and sphinxes. The kittens that lived under the bridges liked the sculptures of Lions. They thought that in some way, the lions were relatives to the cats of St. Petersburg. On summer nights, cats loved to gather on the different embankments of the city.

Once the cats decided to admire how some bridges would be opened. They took sausages with them in case the walk dragged on, and set off along the Neva River. They cheerfully talked and did not see where they were going. Not noticing the road, they went quite far from their house, which was under the Palace Bridge. Then, they passed the University building, and suddenly saw the Academy of Arts.

The "Palace Bridge cats" looked around and realized that the place was not very familiar to them. Nearby was a park. There local cats walked, sniffed flowers and listened to some fairy tales of the old cat Buyan. Then the "Palace Bridge cats" also decided to stay for a short time. From there, it was especially pleasant to admire how the Palace Bridge would be opened. And then, behind their Palace Bridge, they could see the Peter and Paul Fortress with a high gilded spire of the cathedral.

The cats knew that this Peter and Paul Cathedral is the highest in the city, and clearly visible from all sides. Kittens decided that even if any of them get lost, this cathedral will be their guideline, or compass.

On the other side of the river Neva, the majestic St. Isaac's Cathedral stood. It had the round golden dome. So that place for the review was great. The cats are comfortably seating on the granite parapet (fence), which separated the road from the river. They began to look around and discuss the events of the long forgotten centuries, marveling at the wonders of the world.

Next to them cats saw two the most ancient monuments of St. Petersburg - mysterious Sphinxes. Once upon a time in Egypt, many sphinxes adorned the avenue leading to the palace of Amenhotep III. But these Sphinxes on the Neva River were very old. They were more than three and a half thousand years old. Only in the 19th century, these sphinxes were brought to St-Petersburg.

Kitten saw the inscription on their pedestals: "The Sphinx from the ancient Thebes in Egypt was transported to the city of St. Peter in 1832." All kittens were very surprised at this word. Then, they asked the oldest cat Vasily what this would mean. And the cat Vasily told them the tale of the Sphinx.

The terrible winged monster by name Sphinx had the body of a lion, and the face of Pharaoh Amenhotep III. Sphinx guarded his tomb in Egypt.

Once in ancient times, according to the tales of Mythology, the Sphinx stood at the gates of an ancient city called Thebes. No one could enter this city without first solving the riddle of the Sphinx. And the riddle was this:

"Who is walking on four legs in the morning? Then, who walks on two legs in the afternoon, and then, who walks on three legs in the evening?"

The answer to the riddle was simple only for some very well-educated and well-read people. The response was: "In the morning, in the early childhood, this is a child, who is crawling on two feet and two hands (on all fours). 'The Day' is the time, when an adult walks on two legs. And the "Evening" is old age, when an old man might need a cane."

The bloodthirsty Sphinx killed all those who could not solve his riddle. There were fewer people left in the city of Thebes. There was no one who could come in and work making all kinds of goods and products. The city was doomed to death.

But then, one day a very clever wanderer by the name of Oedipus figured out and understood the riddle and what that meant. The Sphinx could not survive that someone was smarter than him. In complete despair, the Sphinx rushed off a cliff and disappeared. And the entrance to the city of Thebes now became free. The grateful and amused city residents chose their savior, the wise Oedipus, as the king of the city. He wisely ruled for a long time.

That was the story the kittens learned from their old friend, the cat Vasily. But there was another wonderful sculpture near the cats on the sides of the granite pier. Two statues of the bronze winged lion - the terrible Griffins, stood almost near the water. The griffins pressed their ears to their heads and maliciously bared their mouths. They guarded the entrance to the

curved grounds with granite benches where the cats were sitting.

Kittens asked big cat Vasily again about these two terrible Griffins. Later cat Vasily will tell more about the meaning of terrible Griffins.

While cat Vasily was talking, kittens got very hungry from many impressions. They began quickly eat their sausages. They wanted to offer some food to the Griffins and Sphinxes. But griffins and sphinxes were only sculptures. And while the cat Vasily was talking about the terrible Griffins, the two huge wings of the Palace Bridge were already fully opened almost upright.

Mommy Murka said that the kittens need to be attentive to what is happening around, and remember what they see when they walk. And she said that there are balls near the embankment at the descent to the Neva River. Once, the master mason Samson Sukhanov by eye knocked out the geometrically accurate balls. He did not use any measuring instruments.

In addition, he knocked them out almost from the first blow. Then one cats climbed onto the ball. He was happy that he was sitting very high and could see everything far around. But the mommy Murka said: "It's time to go home. Let's go back and describe what we saw to those who did not go for a walk today." And the cats went home.

And another time, when cats again went for a walk, they remembered that they were passing the "Spit of Vasilevskiy Island" from the other side. And St. Isaac's Cathedral was still on the opposite bank of the Neva. In summer, a special device was installed under the Neva. During the White Nights it was turned on, and the cats admired the artificial fountain.

In the city on the Neva, there were many magnificent granite parapets (fences) near the Neva. They separated the Neva River from the road. Also, the Neva River had many beautiful cast-iron fences. The cats loved to admire these magnificent cast-iron fences of the magical city. When they were sitting on the University Embankment, they always saw St. Isaac's Cathedral on the opposite bank. For them, this meant that they were not far from their Palace Bridge and could quickly return home.

Griffins

In the magical city of St. Petersburg, the favorite place for the beautiful relaxation on the water is the Griboedov Channel. Sometimes adult cats go boating along the rivers and channels. Another time, they even try to catch some fish while sitting in the boats. And others, who cannot afford such expensive fun, just watched them from above. They were also happily about the cats in the boats. Several ducks would often swim nearby. They were hoping, also, for their own good luck and dream to get the fresh fish for lunch.

The bank bridge across the Griboedov Channel is decorated with massive figures of Mythical creatures - Griffins. Fantastic Griffins have the body and head of a lion, and behind their backs are snow-white eagle wings. In many legends, the Griffins were considered the most reliable guards of the gold pantries, guardians of secrets, treasures and life paths. That is why they were installed on the Bank Bridge. Two proud monsters guarded not only the bridge, but also the gold reserves stored in a nearby bank.

Behind the Bank Bridge, a magnificent view of the "Church of the Savior on Blood" and the Kazan Cathedral opens for everybody enjoyment.

Walks

On fun summer days, mommy - cat Murka dresses everyone up by putting the bow ties on the kittens. And their daddy, big cat Vasily invites his family out for a walk. They might go even farther from their home to the Summer Garden. Just in case, the cautious daddy Vasily, knowing about the variability of the weather in St. Petersburg, carries a huge family umbrella with him. But while the sun is shining, on such a wonderful day, the elder brother takes an interesting book to read aloud to everyone in the park.

Little kittens brought their favorite toys to play in the alley of the park or in the sand box. It is time for fun.

The cat's house is under the Palace Bridge. But the family of cats sometimes goes quite far from their home, almost to the Peter and Paul Fortress. There, under its walls, they sit on the grass and read and play. Everyone is surprisingly pleased to ride and roll on the fresh grass or smell all beautiful flowers. And other cats are watching the happy life of the wonderful family.

When they come to the Summer Garden, there they see the palace of Peter the Great, the founder of St. Petersburg. In such wonderful summer walks, mother Murka sits on a bench and knits winter sweaters for her many children. And another time she reads them Pushkin's fairy tales about the "Cat Scientist" by the name Buyan.

The most intelligent kittens listen to her carefully, and try to understand. But the smallest kittens just play in the sandbox.

After a long walk, all kittens want to eat there, in the park. Their father cat Vasily, as always, brought the delicious sausages for them. His children kittens love sausages.

Other parent cats like to nurse the kittens in the strollers and some enjoy reading a book in the park. The smart parents teach their kittens that it is good to combine the useful things with the pleasant doing.

Promenade

Cats most often walk nearby their home. They like the beautiful embankments. They especially love the Palace and Admiralteyskaya embankment. These embankments are not far from their home, just across the Neva River.

Also, the kittens could see the beautiful "Spit of Vasilevskiy Island" with the main building with white columns. In the 19 century it was the Exchange. And nearby is the red "Rostral columns", which represent the power and grandeur of the Russian navy. On holidays, the torches burn on their peaks. Further to the left of the Rostral columns on the embankment are colorful old buildings of the 18th century. It is the historical and beautiful place, and the intelligent cats love it.

Near the descents to the Neva, on the high granite pedestals are the mysterious regal "Lions" with balls under their feet. Comfortably sitting on a cast-iron "rug", Lions faithfully carry out their service.

These "Beast Kings" have the hugely success with the kittens. All cats are sure that they are very similar to Lions. Adult cats often like to climb on the backs of their distant relatives and rest there in the safety. On warm summer days, cats carried chairs out into the sun. They placed them directly on the granite embankment. Big and adult cats seat and talk, while others read the newspaper.

Older brothers caught a favorite fish in the Neva River. When they got a lot of fish, they cooked the dinner. After the cats eat hearty, they collect a particularly beautiful fish in a jar of water. This is their storehouse and their own "Aquarium." And then, admire it until the next dinner.

Some sea gulls often flew to the cats, and admire their "Aquarium" with the fish. In secret, they wanted to get that easy prey. But the neck of the jar is very narrow. So, the gulls could not get the fish. So, they had to fly away with nothing, and hunt the fish themselves.

PART TWO

Good girl Lila

When mommy Murka was preparing dinner or cleaning her house under the Palace Bridge, she usually kept her kittens in a large box so that they would not run far. Once, the cat Murka invited a very nice neighbor girl Lila to visit her. She even allowed Lila to stroke the kittens.

All kittens were multi-colored handsome, big-eyed, furry and unusually funny. It was evident that they are very curious about everything. Kittens cautiously leaned out of the box, looking around. And then again they hid back in the box, screaming: "Oh, what a huge world there behind the box. Even it is scary to go out, we want to see it." And mommy Murka told her cat Vasily:

"In several weeks it would be nice to find a comfortable house for each kitten"!

One of the kittens was the liveliest. He looked like a gray striped tiger cub. Its silky skin was covered with black and white stripes. A white spot shone on the end of his nose and on his legs. The kitten sat between his relatives, holding his paws over the side of the box.

When a good girl Lila came to visit cat Murka, the kitten looked at the girl Lila. She  could hear him muttering: "Well, you are all considering and considering us. I am better and more beautiful than all. Take me with you already and love me! ". The polite girl Lila asked first the permission from mommy Murka to take a closer look at the kittens. Then, she took one in her arms. After that, she no longer wanted to part with him. Lila put the kitten in a large bag, and carried him to her home.

"Well," said mother Murka, I am glad that one kitten already has found a good home. Maybe other kittens can be successful, as well."

***

New home

Arriving home, Lila opened the lid of her bag. The kitten with the curiosity leaned out from there, looked around and approved of the whole situation. Then he loudly declared: "meow." Cats always understand what people want from them. Although, with the sound of "meow" they never communicate with each other. Their language of communication is hissing, rumbling and snorting. With meowing, they speak only to people, thinking that they speak excellently in human language.

In this case, the cat told everyone around that he urgently needed to eat something to complete his happiness. The girl Lila put some food in a bowl, and set the kitten down for a dinner.

At that time in Russia a very funny children's song was popular in the country. That song was making fun of lazy children. It was like that: "Antoshka-Antoshka! Let's go to dig some potato! And a lazy boy replayed: "Tili-Vali. This job we did not learn at school."

This is why the good girl Lila began to call her little kitten "Antoshka" or simply "Tosha."

The amazing kitten Tosha turned out to be very smart and understood everything on the fly. In addition, he was the neatest cat in the world. Tosha loved in the evenings, before going to his bed to clean himself from all the dirt and bustle of the day. He spent several hours doing this. He was sure, that it was a very necessary thing to do.

***

Cleanliness

From the very first day, the girl Lila decided to watch the cat, helping him to develop the correct behavior. Lila knew that the cleanliness is the key to health. She began to teach

Tosh the most important thing in urban life: how to use a human toilet room. But first, she put a sandbox there for him, and some paper was laid on the floor near the toilet. And also for his short legs, in the same place she put a small bench.

After eating, the Tosha cat went to the toilet room. He began to fuss there, trying to "dig" a hole in the sand for his "need." Girl Lila grabbed him and put on the edge of the toilet. Tosha immediately did all his necessity there and cheerfully jumped off the toilet. Thus, Lila did this several times with him. The kitten quickly learned these lessons. From his childhood Tosha was accustomed to this procedure. Then, he all his life preferred to use only a well-maintained, clean, human's toilet, like any other intelligent person.

For this, Tosha created his own special ritual. He warned everyone in advance about the importance what he is going to do. He announced about it by saying loudly "meow". Then he opened the toilet door by his paw and jumped into the edge of the toilet. After he was done, he demanded that everything be washed away.

He was very angry if a god girl Lila did not do it quickly. Tosha ran around like crazy, jumped on the furniture and everywhere he could get to. By all his appearance he was showing that people should wash off the toilet immediately after him. He tried to tell, that it was important in a cramped apartment that everything around would be very clean and tidy.

***

New rules

Time passed. The good girl Lila and her parents loved the kitten very much. They  allowed him to jump everywhere and to do whatever he wanted. Over time, Tosha got used to it, spoiled, and became very self-confident. Finally, he managed to emphasize that he only allowed people to live next to him in the same apartment, so that they fed him.

Sometimes good girl Lila strictly scolded him, telling Tosha "who rules the ball." But in response, Tosha turned into a home tyrant. He tried to emphasize that everyone needs to remember who the dominant and exclusive race on earth is, namely he is the Tosha cat.

The main joy of the cat Tosha was his food. Like other cats, Tosha was well versed in tastes, distinguished between sour, bitter and salty. This intelligibility was due to a good cat scent and well-developed taste buds in the tongue.

Tosha loved to eat and soon became very fat. He became round like a ball, barely turning over from side to side. In justification, he often repeated that the main thing for a cat to make an elegant pose. Then the figure will look nicer.

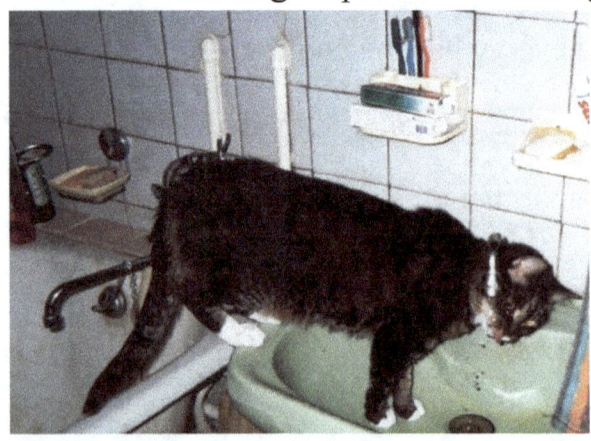 A spoiled cat Tosha loved to eat slowly, with the understanding of this pleasure, carefully chewing food and enjoying every sip. He always looked forward to an hour of feeding. When Tosha was hungry, he simply went up to the table where people were sitting. He repeatedly

emphasized (with a loud meow) the need for his meals at precisely certain hours. He always insisted that discipline in his feeding regimen was very important to him. But when he was sure that nobody sees him, he could pull himself up on his paws and get something off the table.

After a great dinner and all the exciting events of the day, Tosha washed and went to bed. But he snored heavily, and Lila's mother Alena woke him. Tosha was very unhappy about it. He decided to sleep on the feet of his beloved master - the artist Valery. To do this, Tosha went to another room, and there he comfortably settled in the middle of the bed for the whole night. When the owners came to the bedroom, they had to move Tosha to the side. This caused another discontent of cat Tosha. And he thought to himself that the time would come when he would show everyone in the house "who is who" and take revenge.

Cat Revenge

The owners of the cat Tosha worked hard and left him in the house for a long time alone. The obligation to feed him fell on the good girl Lila. But sometimes Lila came back from her school a little later than usual. She missed the time of accurate feeding of her cat.

This led Tosh to an extraordinary rage and vengeful mood. All of his disappointments in the impossibility of the sole rule of the world, he took out on the smallest member of the family, on the good girl Lila.

When it was the time for his lunch, and there was nobody home, Tosha disappointedly sniffed the front door. He felt from afar when Lila was already walking from the elevator to the front door. Of course, she did not expect any bad things or a catch from the seemingly always affectionate kitten. But after hearing her approaching steps, Tosha hid behind the curtain in the hallway and waited. When Lila opened the front door of the apartment, Tosha rushed at her with lightning speed and clung to her legs, like on a tree. He bit furiously and scratched her legs. His attacks were much unexpected for a little schoolgirl.

Once, when the parents came back home in the evening, they found that their daughter Lila was sitting in the bathroom on a heating battery. She managed to slip away from the angry cat there. This was strange, because usually "in public" the cat Tosha tried to seem very meek, affectionate and friendly.

***

Fun Balcony

Cat Tosha constantly lived inside the house, and never went outside. But he was very fond of adventure, hunting and loved height. He climbed all the time somewhere higher than just simple floor. Sometimes in the evening he jumped from the cabinet to the cabinet and, in the end, jumped on the door. From there, he shone on everyone with his mysterious eyes, which were glowing.

The owners knew that the effect of luminous cat eyes can be observed only in the presence of some kind of light source, even the weakest. But Tosha looked menacing. He had a highly developed instinct for the hunter. He was ready to jump on anyone, and he really wanted to hunt.

Watching the growing cat, the owners decided to take him to the veterinarian and make him calmer and easier for everyone. One day good girl Lila and her step father, painter Valery, took Tosha a doctor. A veterinarian did a little surgery on the cat. After that, Tosha stopped doing any physical exercises, did not want to jump on the door.

But Tosha did not calm down immediately. He was a very curious cat, and wanted to smell and try everything. One day, when the balcony door was open, he went there to see what this new place looks like. Finally, the balcony became his favorite place. He spent most of his time philosophizing about life on this fourth-floor balcony. There, from a bird's eye view, Tosha had the opportunity to expand his horizons, comprehend the strange world of the street and watch other cats.

A small glazed balcony with sliding windows was a special place of his privacy and even entertainment. On this balcony, or near the large window of the bedroom, or even leaning out of the window, Tosha was looking for answers to all kinds of the obscure questions that tormented him.

Increasingly, he asked himself, what is he so lacking in life?

Tosha slowly, dreary, secretly dreamed of his own faithful girlfriend, whom he would be caring of. He simply wanted to have at least a comrade or even a whole group of friends with whom he could talk and share the events.

Dreams

One day, Tosha was sitting on a ledge near the large window and looked at the magical city - St. Petersburg. And suddenly he noticed other cats sitting by the window, looking at what was happening outside.

Especially cat Tosha was happy to spot a beautiful cat on the opposite side of the street. The kitty was unusually graceful. Any cat-girl is a queen in the house, so she deserves a worthy name. This kitty was called Asia. Finally Tosha noted, that she often sat by the window, like Tosha, watching life on the river.

One evening, they saw each other. With surprise, they recognized in each other a soul mate. And when they met with admiring eyes, a beautiful silent conversation began between them.

Kitty Asia told Tosha all about the "March Cats". They gather in the spring near her house, often interfere with her sleep. Asia said: "You will also see them and hear their horrible yelling, which they call "singing" in March."

And Tosha told her about his worries and doubts. He shared with Asia that he dreams of an active life and some good friends. Cats perfectly understood each other even at a long distance. They became friends, often waved their paws at the window, and it became much more fun for them to live like that with a company of each other, at least at the window.

When winter came, the balcony was closed tightly. The door to the magic world of the balcony was no longer open. Tosha was looking for a solution to see his friend Asia. So, when no one was home, Tosha went to the window, stretched out and watched what was happening there.

Sometimes he jumped onto the windowsill, where he spent most of his time. But the window looked across the street, from which he could no longer see his beautiful stranger. But he always had the hope that one day he would be able to go outside, in that mysterious and unknown world that he saw from the window or balcony of his house.

The window of the bedroom looked across the street, from which he could no longer see his beautiful friend Asia. Tosha always kept the hope that one day he would be able to go outside. He dreamed to go for a walk in that mysterious and unknown world, that he saw from the window or balcony of his house. He wanted to meet new people and make new friends.

New Year

Tosha saw in the window, that the winter was very cold. There was a lot of snow around, and the Neva River froze. Cat Tosha was a homer cat now. But he heard that the street kittens did not go to the slopes of the Neva River or to the lions.

But still, once Tosha saw that one wonderful family of cats went to the Admiralty Embankment to celebrate the holiday. They took even the smallest kittens with them and showed them sculptures of the mysterious Lions from the frozen Neva. They admired the fireworks, ate sausages, and took a new Christmas tree to someone they planned to visit.

Soon, in the house where Tosha lived, the good girl Lila began to decorate the Christmas tree. Cat Tosha sat nearby and watched her carefully. When everyone went to the store, Tosha decided to try himself as a Christmas tree toy. He went to the Christmas tree and smelled it. Even thought, the artificial green tree did not smell anything special, it was very tall and bewitchingly beautiful. Tosha easily climbed on it, and comfortably settled there among the toys. When the adults returned home, he did not think to get down or say something to them. He played hide and seek.

The girl Lila looked for him and called for him for a long time. But Tosha sat on the tree, hiding. He also sarcastically and sardonically was watching the bustle and concern of his owners. He just thought: "Now you know how it feels to be locked up all the time. I want to be free! " Then, parents were very surprised when they finally spotted a kitten among Christmas toys. That evening Tosha received a festive plate of fish, which he loved very much.

March cats

As it turned out later, Tosha believed that all his behavior problems were explained by painful stress in the veterinarian office in his early childhood. Indeed, shortly after his appearance in the house, Tosha was taken to the hospital. The veterinarian performed a small operation for him so that the kitten would not turn into a more aggressive cat later and would not constantly screaming as any other straight "March cat".

At the beginning of every spring, the lazy "March Cats" roamed the streets of St. Petersburg. They did not want to study or work, but they were looking for an easy life. In the evenings, they screamed heart-endingly about all kinds of problems in the public life of the city. They were not ashamed to shout their meaningless songs at all not in musical, but in disgusting voices. Standing under the ancient Petersburg lantern, they begged for at least some, even very skinny, but still free fish. And then, if they did not get the free meal, they turned everything upside down, putting everyone on their ears, and rushed about in search of grooms and brides.

Cat Tosha watched the "March Cats" from his balcony. He was surprise of such useless wasting their time, and did not want to be anything like them at all. He had no desire to be dating the opposite sex. He considered it all complete nonsense. Tosha was spending all his free time on the balcony or by the window, licking and cleaning his smooth coat. However, once, when the owners came home, Tosha walked to them to their kitchen. There he sat comfortably closer to the table and looked at people with his large gray eyes. But not having received answers to all his silent questions, he began to sigh loudly and defiantly. With all his appearance, Tosha showed that it was the adults who were to blame for the inferiority of his limited balcony of life.

Cat 's Flights

From the first day in the new home, Tosha loved not only the balcony time. He also and most of all liked to pay special attention to the man of the house - Valery, who was living there. Valery was an artist and most often spent time in the house, as did Tosha. The artist painted, and Tosha liked to smell his oil paints. Tosha spent a huge amount of time on the knees or on the shoulder of the artist, helping him to paint.

To everything else, Tosha was a risky cat and craved an adventure. People say that a cat has nine lives. Three life cat plays, three life cats wanders, and the remaining three life cat remains in one place. Cat Tosha demonstrated precisely these qualities of cats.

It seemed that cat Tosha was not afraid or did not understand the height at all. When the passion of hunting and the dream of traveling and finding the friends prevailed over him, Tosha leaned far out of the window, looking around. And sometimes he even tried to walk along the ledge, like a circus performer, without any insurance, easily balancing on narrow crossbars.

One day, fearless cat Tosha demonstrated to all of it to his parents. Being carried away and following the birds, Tosha sometimes tried to take off, which was a great test for him. It also took away a lot of his strength, but not because it was dangerous to fly from that height without a parachute. But because when gravity pulled him down and returned to the ground, Tosha suddenly found himself in an unfamiliar and even hostile environment. After landing, he was in a state of complete and deep shock. So, he quickly hid under the stairs of the basement or under the porch.

The good girl Lila and the artist Valery jumped out of the house, and run in a panic to find the "pilot". They searched and called Tosha for several hours in the rapidly approaching darkness. But Tosha did not want to answer their calls. He feared to attract the attention of some enemies. And the owners of Tosha thought that the main reason for his silence was that the cat was trying to make everyone suffer and worry a little longer. He was sure that in his fall from such a cozy and safe, as it always seemed to him, balcony, there was only their fault. So, he punished the owners by his silence.

After the first such flight from the fourth floor and the fear experienced, Tosha stayed away from the balcony for some time. But the temptation to catch a bird was very high, and everything was repeated from the beginning. His owners still found Tosha and brought the frightened and hushed kitten home. And then they thoroughly washed him in the bath.

Typically, cats did not like to swim. But at the moments of returning to the comfort and safety of his house, Tosha endured everything. He was very grateful to everyone for his sensitivity and concern for him. Grateful for his return, the prodigal cat jumped to the owner of the artist on his shoulder and purred something affectionate in his ear. And then he settled down comfortably on his lap and fell asleep sweetly there. Tosha's quiet, purring sound, and sometimes even the snoring of the kitten, filled the house with comfort and tranquility. And most importantly, Tosha gave everyone a sense of the importance of such stability, reliability and warmth.

Over time, everyone began to think that Tosha's flights were not in vain. He even dreamed to go out and being on the roof. There, it seemed, all cats found the wisdom of centuries. And they were convinced that all animals and all people, regardless of their position or material status, all-all belong to only one earth and only one single moon.

Sometimes, Tosha watched the fireworks outside the window. It made him especially happy. He thought the fireworks done purposefully in his honor or his achievements. Then, he exclaimed: "My flights from the balcony are not just a desire to catch a bird. I strive to overcome the gravity of the earth. My wings are my dreams. My grandmother told me: "Strive to the moon. Then you will most likely find yourself among the Stars ..."

***

Help

The main feature of Tosha's character was his desire to be useful. He strove to serve his masters with everything he could. He wanted to show that he "not without a reason eats their bread." Sometimes his owners even thought that before his cat life, Tosha was most likely a waiter. At least, Tosha was deeply convinced that he should be the main breadwinner of the family. So, he wanted to get at least some food for the household. Usually in the spring he opened the hunting season on his own balcony.

The good girl Lila woke up early. She was getting ready for her school while watching Tosha. Often in the morning Tosha was trying to catch a bird outside the window. In winter, the window was closed. But Lila put the food for the birds outside the big window. And Tosha spent all day at the window. Now he was very busy having fun, even trying to catch the birds through the glass. At least, he did not wake up mother Alena ahead of time.

After intensive attempts and hunting for birds, Tosha slept well all night, and went out only for his breakfast. This meant he had good constant exercise.

Tosha had many talents, but hunting was his main and most successful hobby. Early in the morning, long before the rise of all the household members, he already brought them a caught sparrow. Usually, Tosha laid this already lifeless sparrow on the bed near by the head of the mistress of the house, mother Alena.

And then, Tosha sat down next to her hear and waited when Alena would wake up. He was sure, that she would be very happy about the already prepared breakfast. It was very important to Tosha that mother Alena would immediately see the caught sparrow. Tosha expected her would be very happy about it, and appreciated his desire to be useful. He wanted to see Alena always cheerful, smiling, and not scolding him all the time. Then Tosha would be happy, as well. Several times, Alena explained to Tosha that, in principle, she does not like fresh sparrows. But like all autocrats of the highest race, he was very stubborn and confident in his innocence. Tosha did not listen to her arguments, but continued to bring birds. He was pointing out to everyone his personal usefulness in their family.

While watching cat Tosha, everyone learn many interesting things. For example, when the cat was located near some kind of heat source, everyone in the house was preparing for a cold snap. Everyone noticed the weather getting worse after Tosha slept in the shape of a glomerulus or constantly trying to hide his nose. He was just a weather barometer.

***

Train

Spending many hours on the balcony, Tosha more and more felt that he needed an active social life. He desired to unwind, to see the world and life of other countries. Well, if not countries, then, at least get to know better life in Russian resort places. Tosha was curious to find out how other cats live, whether their owners are good, and how they feed them on the vacation.

His owners saw Tosha's desire to learn more about the world. They feared Tosha's new unpleasant or aggressive actions. The owners took him to a vacation on the Black Sea. Tosha was inspired by such an unusual event, about which he had long dreamed. He hoped that the resort social life would bring him much pleasure, joy and exciting occasions. Then, everyone packed their bags and went to the train station.

In Soviet times in Russia during 1970-1990th the passenger trains were not a very convenient way to travel. But it was just an incredible event, if people had the need to move somewhere else with their pets.

First of all, for such trip with pets, people required to have a special medical certificate for every living creature. This was the medical evidence that all of their pets were healthy, had all the necessary vaccines given on time. Knowing this, the owners of Tosha stocked up with all the necessary information in advance. They naively believed that this was the most important thing for the trip.

When Tosha's family came to the station, they saw that there was a huge line to get in the car. This line moved very slowly. A disheveled and crumpled conductor looked like she wanted to bite everyone. But Tosha's family even from afar tried to joyfully smile at her. An artist Valera, mother Alena, the good girl Lila and even cat Tosha showed with all their looks that they were all right. Their body language expressed that there was nothing to take from them. In general, it would be difficult to find any fault to punish them.

The smart Tosha always tried to help his family. Therefore, when the nasty conductor began to check their tickets, Tosha quickly hid in the large basket. This huge basket was so far empty, and specially stocked for the return trip. Family planned to put in it some delicious fruits when they would go back from the Black Sea to the northern and cold St. Petersburg.

But the conductor tormented by the hangover, noticing the cat Tosha, darted into the basket, suddenly and hysterically cried out that this cat should have a muzzle. The Tosha's brilliant trick of hiding was clearly not a success. At the same time, the line of people around the car was very worried. People were looking

around and asking who was preparing to attack them. Here Tosha's family realized that this, of course, was a trick of the bureaucracy. The drunken conductor had a desire to get some present or a bribe. Then, the artist Valera quickly put some money in her pocket for a hangover.

Observing all this disgrace, the honest Tosha was really very upset. He did not like the conductor. Tosha's concerned how awful it might be on the same train for three days with such conductor, and somehow to get from her the legitimate tea. Tosha thought, that this trip did not portend any pleasure or comfort.

That stressful situation for Tosha was exacerbated by other reasons. Entering the car, the whole family was sandwiched into the narrow space of a small compartment. After a while, Tosha came out of the basket, but felt very constrained and claustrophobic in a confined space.

Anyway, Tosha already missed his favorite balcony. He also, missed the beautiful and clean apartment, where he ate sitting at the table, like all decent people. And here in the train car no one cooked his favorite fish for him at the right time. As a result, Tosha was angry with the whole world. He defiantly refused to eat canned food. Most importantly, he did not want to go to the stinky and dirty public toilet in the vestibule of the train. The artist Valery tried to put some paper on the floor there for the convenience of the cat-esthete. But this caused even greater indignation of the neat cat Tosha.

In the end, in protest against such inhuman conditions for traveling long distances, Tosha went on a hunger strike. Two days later, everyone finally arrived at the final train route, to Novorossiysk. This city was forty kilometers from Gelendzhik, where everyone went for a vacation. As soon as the basket with the cat was put on the platform, a huge pool of his three-day patience appeared from under it. Tosha in this way marked the new territory. Then, all things went easier for him. The family took a taxi and on a steep mountain road in just an hour they reached the house in Gelendzhik. They came to their dear grandmother Anna.

***

Arrival

Tosha family went directly to the grandmother Anna in Gelendzik. It was not too far from the Black Sea, and the house was surrounded by a fantastic garden. When the family and cat Tosha entered the yard, grandmother was very surprised to see such a large company. But Grandmother Anna was a very kind woman, and was happy to have her guests. But it was especially surprising to her that the cat Tosha traveled by train from far away, from St. Petersburg. But she received everyone, as always, with great love. Then, she settled them all in a summer room with a terrace.

Her house was very old and poor, with no hot water. The toilet was far in the yard, as a little shed. But one thing was good. This room had a separate exit to the courtyard. It was pleasant for everyone, because it gave the independence for everybody.

After everyone settled in a new place, Tosha demanded to cook him some fish. As a creature who loved to control everything, he sat right next to the electric stove and watched carefully what people were doing. He wanted that everything was done correctly and in his taste. A hungry cat smelled the cooking fish and licked his lips. And the strongest smell of his favorite food was spreading throughout the district, notifying all neighbors of his safe arrival in the resort town.

Soon after eating a delicious meal and washing himself, Tosha took a little nap in the warm southern sun. Then, he remembered the main reason for his arrival to the south and decided to stretch his legs.

Tosha strove for something interesting and maybe even the most incredible. Dragging his warm tummy with a fish that had just got there, the inexperienced adventurer resolutely stepped into the unknown, into the dark neighboring bushes.

Unexpected

The owner of that area near the grandmother's house was the self-confident orange cat Vasily. He was incredibly surprised by the unexpected invasion of capital's cat Tosha on his territory. The local bandit cat Vasily enjoyed unquestioned authority among local cats. He had long established his firm order, in which no one had the right to doubt, fearing his claws and teeth.

The hungry cat Vasily watched from behind the bushes for the unexpected arrival of a new family with a cat Tosha. He inhaled the aroma of boiled fish, was surprised that such a delicacy as capelin, hake and cod were bought for the new cat. And the orange cat Vasily terribly envied the wealth of the new cat Tosha richness.

Unaware of any catch from the local cats, Tosha amiably walked forward. He did not notice anything dangerous. Wanting to simply empty his intestines, he began to dig a hole near the neighboring bushes. And suddenly he was insidiously attacked from behind by a shameless local cat.

In fairness, it should be said, that orange cat Vasily was not a lean or fit athlete. He also loved to eat "what God will give." He also loved sleeping. And according to his needs he usually was sending his wards everywhere to provide some food for him. But Vasily was cunning. He used the insidious factor of surprise that played into his hands.

After an incredibly unexpected attack, Tosha lost his balance and fell. But then he quickly remembered how he jumped in St. Petersburg from behind a hitch on the good but late for his dinner girl Lila. And, he remembered how he jumped on the balcony to catch the birds. So, Tosha jumped like a ball, released his claws and began to fight back. And the local red-haired cat Vasily, even having fallen, continued to shove his legs from the "lying" position.

***

Tosha's Victory

Tourist cat Tosha and local orange cat Vasily fought for some time with varying success. Both were weighed down by their weighty tummies. But then the courageous cat Tosha began to seem to win. After all, he was well trained in St. Petersburg in his jumping from the fourth floor and flying after the birds. In addition, Tosha often watched various fighting techniques on TV. So, then he finally decided to use his knowledge.

Local cat Vasily had no chance. He could not bear the fatal blow of Tosha's shaggy paw of rage. Feeling that he was losing, the insidious Vasily, first looked around. But since nobody watched his fight with Tosha, Vasily not noticing the public, ran away.

But it was not in the bizarre nature of local cat Vasily to forgive his loss. Vasily decided to defeat Tosha under the other circumstances, which would be more favorable to him. In the circle of his friends, he began to conduct propaganda against "wealthy visitors, snickering fish with unknown names." Vasily tried to seduce his rogue friends by telling them, if they would defeat Tosha, they will be able to take possession of all these good fish that Tosha eat all the time.

The next night local cat Vasily called his gang of cats. They all always were eternally hungry cats, and ready to fight for free food. Therefore, they made an ambushed near by the house, where cat Tosha stayed. They were waiting for the next good moment of Tosha's appearance. The naïve cat Tosha was inspired by his first victory. He longed for a new sensation of resort social life. The next day, he decided to continue his adventures on the Black Sea.

***

Feline art

In St. Petersburg, good girl Lila and her family often watched their cat Tosha. They learned that he could sort the noise in the different directions. The hearing of cats is generally well developed.

As a solitary hunter, a cat is still a social animal. Cats use a wide range of sound signals for communication, as well as smells, hormones and body movements. Cats are able, with their eyes closed, to navigate in any space. With each ear cats could move independently, turning it almost 180° in different directions, and simultaneously watching two sources of sound. Amazingly, cats can recognize the strength of a sound, its removal and pitch, and accurately determine its location. They could hear the rustle and squeak, and by that little noise they could catch the mice running by.

Tosha decided to demonstrate all these unique qualities to the local Gelendzhik cats. He was still a little snob, and his ambitions prevented him from enjoying life without competing with others.

***

Next nights

The second evening came, the good girl Lila let Tosha out into the yard for doing his necessity. He demonstrated as if he was trying to dig a hole for his toilet in the garden dirt. Then, he looked back at his owner. Suddenly Tosha rushed with all his might towards the neighbors.

Lila regretted that she did not tie her adventurer to the foot of the bed, or did not put a leash for him, like on dogs. She regretted that she did not keep him at home. But it was too late.

Tosha spent that night in a fierce battle with the local cats over the problem who would to control now that territory. And then for another two nights in a row, the restless sleep of the neighbors was accompanied by wild battle cries and the fierce battles of local cats. But maybe this time, they fought for the attention of a local beauty.

On the third night, the Tosha family had almost lost their hope that their tender and unexperienced cat Tosha would survive in these battles or return home. They continued to call him all day, but he did not come. In the end, firmly convinced that their cat's love of boiled fish would bring him home, they began to cook fish from morning to evening. Tosha owners were sure that this overwhelming smell (from which the whole family was already sick) would lead even a half-dead Tosha back home.

Finally, Lila who was standing at the gate saw Tosha barely moving along the street. He was badly battered, but not defeated. He was dirty, having lost half of his skin, but he looked wise. Tosha looked as if he now learned the imperfection of the world. And most importantly, this was not the world he dreamed about for long St. Petersburg nights. For Tosha, this real world in the Black Sea town was full of cunning and unpleasant surprises. It was a world where there was a fierce struggle for spheres of influence. The winners were those who had more friends, better prepared plans, deep thoughts or better designed tricks. It looked like, only the cunning, strong and treacherous could win.

The sophisticated, but not broken romantic Tosha spent the remaining days of his vacation high on the roof of the house. There high on the roof, he was closed from all prying eyes by apricot trees. It was a convenient position where he calmly lay in the sun, licking his battle wounds. Tosha was now sure that it was much safer and more pleasant to watch other people's high life from above. And it's better to do it from afar. As a touring stranger, he was not accepted into the public life of the local revels, where they were not even fed for free. Yes, he no longer aspired to this paradise. The vacation on the Black Sea brought him a disappointment. It seemed to be pointless. During this turbulent epic, Tosha dreamed to come back to his comfortable past life. Now he believed in the meaning and value of what he had before, and valued his past life even more.

Returned

In the end of August, the Tosha's family returned from the Black Sea to St. Petersburg. Tosha saw from the height of his window a park near St. Isaac's Cathedral. The cathedral shone with its golden domes in the rare autumn sun.

There were still cats gathering and discussing their summer trips and adventures. Tosha would also like to take a walk there and share her adventures in the south. But in St. Petersburg he was not allowed to go out.

The city was already quite cool, it was raining endlessly and the winds were blowing. In anticipation of winter, the windows on the balcony did not open. And soon they were tightly screwed up for warmth, pasted over with paper. Now Tosha no longer walked on the ledge, but simply sat by the glazed window and looked at the gray sky, where even birds almost did not appear.

The time of his beloved hunt has passed, and he again felt loneliness and boredom. After all, everyone needs to communicate with their own kind. Tosha saw from the window that some cats are friends with dogs and even walk together. Sometimes it seemed to him that cats brought dogs up as their own pets, and even brought dogs out for a walk on a leash. And he also dreamed of somehow getting a puppy - a friend.

In the evening, when his family was returning from work, he jumped onto the shoulder of his beloved master Valery. Tosha rubbed his ear and whispered something mournfully to him. It was clear that he was complaining that the family was not paying him enough attention.

Then Tosha sat down next to Valery nearby his easel. And while Valery was drawing, Tosha continued to talk to him. Tosha began to recall all different faults of Lila and mother Alena. He blamed them for all his problems and the life, locked inside the fourth walls.

It turned out that Tosha felt generally an unrecognized genius. He thought that his family neglected to recognize all his talents. He recalled that mother Alena refused to consume his fresh sparrows. He recalled that Lila did not come home on time to give him his favorite fish. And the most importantly, the family was guilty that they subjected him to severe trials in the train and during the South vacation.

As a result, from the endless Tosha's meows and purrs, his family realized that Tosha clearly expressed a desire to take care of someone. He did not find self-satisfaction in those around him. He was too lonely while his loving relatives spent most of the day outside the home. Tosha wanted to have a loyal friend with whom he would spend the whole day together. He even dreamed that maybe he would even share his fish with him for a dinner.

Tosha clearly needed a true and loving friend who respected and appreciated him. Every day cat Tosha looked more and more unhappy. It was the time to help him. Then having discussed everything, the family found an original way to do this. They bought a little German shepherd puppy. The new and happiest page of Tosha's life has arrived.

***

PART THREE

Solution

Once upon a time, cat Tosha was born in the magical city of St. Petersburg. The good girl Lila took him to her apartment and raised him. Tosha never left it, and only from time to time flew after the birds from the balcony, which was on the fourth floor. He just dreamed about some active social life. Then, the good girl Lila and her parents took Tosha to a vacation. After several days in a very uncomfortable train, they visited grandmother house in Gelendzhik on the Black Sea. There Tosha met some bold bully, local bandit cats. He fought fiercely for his life.

After defeating a local Gelendzhik cat, Tosha believed that now he was a real hero. He felt like he was an unrecognized genius. Tosha was sure that the whole world should already

have known about his adventures. When he returned back home to St. Petersburg, he was expecting some respectful signs of attention. "Well, everyone could at least read about it somewhere or see on TV,"- thought Tosha.

A trip to the southern resort and a battle in the grandmother's garden with local cats taught Tosha a lot. But the main quality of all people, the modesty was not increased in him yet. But the memory of these incredible events for a long time did not let the cat Tosha sleep peacefully.

He sometimes reminded his beloved artist Valery, that the mistress of the house, mother Alena, refused to eat the fresh sparrows, which he so successfully caught on the ledge and brought for her. Then, he recalled that the good girl Lila often came back from her school too late, and missed his specific feeding time. And the most importantly, the cat believed that the family took him far south, against his own free will, without asking him.

However, before all of that, Tosha often dreamed about the high life and longed for some adventures. Details about the fascinating life of the cat Tosha read in the Book 1 and Book2 of this trilogy.

Finally, the owners realized why Tosha has his endless "meows". He clearly needed to take care of someone. He had few relatives who loved him, but they spent most of the day at work and at school. Tosha dreamed of having a loyal friend with whom he would share the whole day together. Tosha even once thought that he might be would be able to share his fish with a friend.

He saw from the window of his house that other cats had their own pets - dogs. So Tosha started to dream about a puppy who would become his faithful friend and participant in the games. Tosha was sure that he could take care of the puppy.

Every day the cat Tosha looked more and more unhappy. It was the time to help him. Then having discussed everything, the family found an original way to do this. They bought a little German shepherd puppy Break. This is where the new, happiest page of Tosha's life began.

***

Puppy

When the puppy arrived from Germany, the artist Valery and the girl Lila went to the rail station to meet new family member. Mistress of the house, mother Alena with her cat Tosha was waiting for them at home, in a warm and comfortable apartment.

The puppy was marvelous and cute. In his passport, that came with him, his name "Break" was written in black and white. Break looked like a very smart and all understanding dog. He had long and clean pedigree. His breed was among the best in the dog family.

Everyone at home was extremely pleased with the new member of the family with such a strange name. At first, Tosha was also very happy. He was even inspired by a sudden change in his boring life. Amazingly, Tosha was not even jealous of the puppy. Even thought, most of the family attention turned mainly to a tiny and clumsy Break. The generous and already mature Tosha forgave everybody for everything. All this turmoil that the funny and fat puppy created, was exiting for him, as well.

In addition, the puppy Break was very kind by nature. He was constantly pleased with everything and everyone around him. Because of his excessive friendliness, the dog constantly wagged her tail. First Tosha, who was wised by his last summer vacation experience, perceived this dog gesture as a sign of aggression. It led him to some tension and his readiness to repel the attack. Only much later Tosha learned completely different dog language. They adapted to understand each other with the help of the master.

***

Tosha and Break

People say that some humans live "like a cat and a dog", referring to the implacable hostility between these breeds. It happens. But there are many cases with the opposite situations. For example, one old folk tale tells describes how a hunter lost a mitten in the winter. And then different animals found refuge in it. They, out of need, lived in peace and harmony, never quarreling.

Once the good girl Lila showed fun drawing by E. Rachev to her pets, and said: ". Look, how friendly you need to live!"

The friendship between Tosha and Break was created from their early childhood. At the time when the two month old puppy came to the family, Tosha was almost two years old. From early childhood they lived in the same apartment together. It was important for the peace and happiness of all households to have friendship between all members of the family. In addition, like all children, the cat and the puppy watched their owners. They observed all who lived nearby, and adopted the characters of their owners. Seeing the kindness and love of people, smart pets did not want to conflict.

The main cause of the hostility between cats and dogs is the different body language. In St. Petersburg apartment attentive owners of cat Tosha and dog Break taught them to understand each other. Especially Lila tried hard to help her pets to be respectful to each other.

She told Tosha that their dog Break wagging tail means greeting. And she explained to her dog, that if cat Tosha curved his back, it means that he is very angry. At such moments, it is better to leave him alone. The girl taught the puppy that in cats, wagging the tail means irritation, unlike in dogs. And from the balcony she showed a black cat, which stood there with a curved back, ready to fight.

And then Tosha added that cats can also bend their backs and rumble when they feel good and pleased, especially when someone strokes them. At such moments, Tosha approached his main owner, the artist Valery, rubbed his foot, expressing that it was the time to cares him.

So, living together from an early age, the cat Tosha and the dog Break learned to talk to each other. And then they began to be very good friends and adapt to each other's body language. After all, people also learn not only foreign languages of other countries, but also the foreign language of animals.

***

Cleanliness

Cat Tosha had an obsession with the cleanliness. He expected that the girl Lila will teach the dog Break some good manners. Tosha meant that the dog should learn also how to use the comfortable "human" toilet. But in the first days of his stay in the apartment, the puppy Break did all his "necessities" right on the floor. Soon Tosha noticed that the dog was creating too much new work for everybody, including himself. The owner of the house, the artist Valery, did not have the time to run out with the puppy from the fourth floor to the street for all dogs' natural affairs. So where this "necessity" found the puppy, there he did it all – on the floor.

And the clean-up Tosha walked behind the puppy and tried to immediately clean and bury everything. But nothing disappeared. So, Tosha run to Lila and asked her to remove it right away. After several days of unsuccessful struggle for cleanliness, Tosha was exhausted and defeated. He could not even stand on his feet from fatigue, and he began to have an allergy. Tosha simply stopped moving on the floor, it was already above his dignity. He started jumping from cabinet to cabinet. And then he found a warm place on the washing machine. There, height up, he was waiting when the difficult time of the dog adaptation to the cleanliness would be finished.

***

In the meantime, let's learn a wisdom that will help to understand the difference between a cat and a dog. "If the tail of the cat is at rest, then your cat is calm. Suddenly he swings his tail, which means he is nervous. In the dogs the opposite is true. The tail plays a different role. And therefore, so often the cats do not understand the dog's body language. But I'll tell you a secret; there is no stronger cat-dog friendship. If people were friends like some cat and dog, everyone around the world would only live in peace".

Respect

Soon, Tosha began to notice more and more that his family was paying special attention to the little puppy. Moreover, they all forgive him for everything he did. At that time, cat Tosha decided to emphasize his superiority. He felt that he must to emphasize that in this apartment, he is the "navel of the earth." Tosha considered a puppy of Break was his ward. The cat Tosha began to walk around with his tail lifted. He was expressing confidence and firmness of his character with all its appearance. It did not make much effect on the kind Break, who already accepted Tosha as he was, with all narcissism and pride.

Then, Tosha more and more often began to tell the naive puppy about his adventures in Gelendzhik with the local robber cats. Soon, Break was convinced that Tosha was the real hero. This was a very happy moment for Tosha. He wanted that puppy clearly understood his authority in the house.

But soon cat Tosha got more concern. The puppy also loved to eat, and especially he admired the fish. For a cat, it was his favorite and the most pleasant time. But the dog Break ate very fast, just swallowing everything at once. Tosha did not keep pace with the dog, and decided to establish the boundaries of the permissible. From day one, Tosha refused to get his food on the same plate with the dog. But no matter what, Lila tried to bring the cat and dog closer. She fed them at the same time, placing plates close in the corner of the kitchen. In the beginning, Lila even stood by their side and observed that everything was peaceful and pleasant. She prevented cat from hiss at little dog.

Dog Break quickly and carefully licked and cleaned the bottom of his bowl. After that, the puppy laid next to the cat's bowl, periodically licking his lips, and watched how cat was eating. He was squinting at the cat and whispered that the food is more important for the growing organism of the dog, than for the lazy slacker cat. But cat Tosha ate, turning his head slightly to the left, then to the right, and did not listen to the dog's grumbles.

Once Brake, seizing the moment and put his face in a cat's bowl. But cat Tosha was on his guard. After he gained an extensive experience in his vacation on the Black Sea, Tosha knew how to fend for himself. In response, he painfully grabbed the dog in the nose. The girl Lila stood nearby and immediately shamed Tosha. But the cat explained that this was just a small warning to an expensive, but still ungrateful family member. Unsuspecting puppy Break was simply stunned by such a rebuff. He never again touched the cat's bowl.

But sometimes Tosha run faster and came to his boll before the dog. After eating all he had, he would hide the rest of the fish behind his back. Then he sat as if he did not know anything. But at the same time Tosha watched whether the dog Break would look for a fish behind him. For cat Tosha, the main thing was to show the young ignoramus that it was impossible to touch somebody else things. Seeing that the noble dog did not touch his fish without his permission, satisfied cat laid down in the middle of the room. Then, he started to teach Break to be more restrained in the food consumption. By this time Tosha himself already looked like a round ball, but considered himself moderately fit.

Before going to his bed, cat Tosha repeated some words: "If you are fat and clumsy, take at least some elegant poses. This golden rule is known even to cats."

Due to a not very active and not very eventful life, and also because of the cold Russian climate, the cat and the dog were always very hungry. They tried to beg for food, or get it wherever they could, even sometimes used illegal way.

One day, there were some butter, cheese, sausage and other wonderful delicacies were stored in the refrigerator. Cat Tosha convinced the dog that it is all right to open the door without the permission of the adults and get it all for a dinner. Naive and hungry Break firmly believed in the wisdom and superiority of the cat. Break was easily succumbed to his manipulations.

One day, when no one was home, Break opened this seductive refrigerator. The dog could not resist the seductive smell which was coming from that white big thing - refrigerator. They both fast ate the monthly supply of food. Then the dog Break remembered that he was forbidden to even come close to this white box with the delicious smell. But the arguments of the cat, who promised to take all the blame on himself, quickly convinced the dog's stomach grumbling from the hunger.

Later in the evening, Break felt completely out of place. His stomach was swollen and he fell ill. In fear, the dog hid under the desk and fell asleep. When everyone returned from work, he did not rush to meet the hosts, as usual. He did not lean out from there even at their cheerful call. He felt deeply guilty and could not tell that the cat was to blame. Then he finally came out, tail down under his legs, looking somewhere to the side. But his masters quickly forgave him, although they remained hungry themselves for a long time.

***

Games

Despite their age, everyone in the house loved to play some games. It was especially good to do after the dinner on weekends. They all enjoyed playing mostly hide and seek and catch-up. Everyone was hiding, and dog Break was looking. He quickly found everyone in small three-room bedroom apartment. At first, Break did not understand the game well, but learn fast. Then, he was carried away by the game. He especially loved when somebody threw his small ball into the back room. He ran there, found a toy, brought it, and waited to be treated with something good.

Joint games brought together all members of the family, both people and animals. Games brought great pleasure to everyone. After these hectic runs around the apartment, soon everyone calmed down, realizing that it was time for everyone to do their own thing. And then they all cleaned and went to sleep.

In mother Alena's apartment of St. Petersburg was rare, but peaceful cat-dog world. All family members, mistress Alena, artist Valery, girl Lila, Tosha and Break tried to do everything together and played a lot. Soon, the cat and the dog began to greet each other with their noses, and increasingly sleep in an embrace. The main thing was to pay equal attention to everybody. Because where there is no equality, there can be no friendship.

Only Tosha had his own idea of what the friendship of a dog and a cat means. He did not forget to remind Break that the cats belong to St. Petersburg Lion family, and generally divine family. Although Break was growing every day, he was still a very young puppy. One day when he arrived to this house, he found the cat already living there as a dominant leader. Then, cat Tosha taught Break that he was a hero at the Black Sea fight. So, Break believed in it, too. Dog Break loved Tosha under any circumstances. On whatever cat

Tosha said to him, noble dog just replied that he was simply an ordinary German shepherd, whose role is to serve his people.

But Break had one, but the most important advantage, which Tosha greatly appreciated. A loyal dog walked with the owner, artist Valery, outside the house. But Tosha could not persuade anyone to let him go for a walk on the street.

**

Winter

So the first winter for Break came with its frosts and snowstorm. His owner Valery had to take the dog out twice a day. Especially Break loved morning walks with Valery.

The dog felt good and confident next to his adored owner. If Break walked with girl Lila or with mistress Alena, but suddenly saw his master on the street, then his joy knew no bounds. It was hard to keep him on the leash. Dog Break was very strong. He could drug anybody a few meters on the snow. Then, Break would reach his master Valery and would be happy. Then he jumped on his chest and licked him happily.

More than anything, Break loved their walks in the wasteland. At six o clock in the morning other dog's comrades appeared in muzzles and on leashes there. Break, cheerfully, with a loud bark, ran after them through snowdrifts and mud. Even though Break was young, he was already huge and courageous dog. He did not find anything dangerous for himself outside the house.

And when Brake returned from a street walk, cat Tosha joyfully ran to him. The cat carefully sniffed the dog from head to toe, studying what interesting Brake brought with him, in addition to the fleas. Tosha longed to know all the news that was outside, in a dangerous and difficult world for him. This was the world of fears and surprises about which Tosha had known some time ago. He learned about it in his vacation journey to the south. Only sometimes, before going to bed, Tosha spoke about his adventures on the Black Sea to the faithful friend Break. And they fell asleep, embracing under this strange tale. But first, after any walk, Break was accustomed to be washed. When he returned from his walk outside,

he rushed into the bathroom and jumped into the bath. The bathroom was immediately covered with the dirt from the top to the bottom. And Break was waiting for his master Valery to wash him thoroughly. Then, the dog jumped out just as quickly from there, briskly shook himself, dousing everything around. Then, he also rushed cheerfully into the kitchen, sliding on the floor, and wanting to quickly see what was prepared for his dinner there. And Valery had to clean that human bath after his beloved dog.

Break always finished his dinner very quickly, although a cat hissed around him. But Brake did not pay attention at all to this hissing. After all these exciting joys on the street, he lay on the bedding under the master's table and slept immediately.

Tosha's Hobby

One day Tosha started a new hobby and followed this for a long time. Trying to show Break that cleanliness in the house is his main priority, Tosha tried to clean the dog with his little tongue. When Break came from a walk, Tosha jumped onto the dog's huge head. He clung tightly to Break's skin so that the dog would not run away. Tosha licked huge face of the dog, trying to make him perfectly clean. But he did not have enough saliva for the huge face of the dog. This face was already almost the same size as the size of the cat. In addition, Tosha quickly got tired, and he also needed to wash himself afterwards.

All these new worries and problems really angered Tosh. Therefore, unable to cope with the incredibly time-consuming task of washing the dog's face, Tosha bit his nose slightly. It was indicating that it would be better for the dog to wash himself. But Break was not only extremely kind, but also a patient dog. He thought it was some kind of special game or a tradition of his new home. The dog patiently endured all the washes done by the cat with inevitability.

The lessons that Tosha cat gave about the cleanliness did not go in vain. After all of Tosha's effort, having endured all the cat's procedures, Break carefully took Tosha's small head into his huge mouth and licked it gently, playing with him.

Although Tosha was very tiny compared to the dog, he was older and wiser than the puppy. And indeed, life under one roof for all intelligent beings should have been as pleasant and comfortable as possible. The main thing in a good relationship is the ability to give in to each other and adapt to the habits of others. Animals understood this well and never quarreled.

***

Be useful

When the puppy Break appeared in the house, Tosha decided that the dog should be useful for something. When the winter came, Tosha started a new tradition. Once after the dinner, Tosha jumped on the dog back and stayed there to be warm. Break did not mind. So they spent many nights together. Sometimes the cat wanted to emphasize again that he was the master in the house. So, Tosha came to the room, where the dog slept, and laid down on the dog special mattress under the table. Most likely, Tosha was simply pretending to be sleeping. Tosha stealthily glanced at the dog, slightly opening one eye. Then, the dog would come to his place under the table, saw that the impudent Tosha already "sweetly sleeping." In the dog's sincerity, Break did not have the strength to disturb his friend cat. He modestly squeezed himself closer to him, barely fitting in the same small mattress.

In winter, in the apartment was quite cold. Most often, Tosha slept between the master's bed and barely warm central heating battery. But the cat did not allow the dog to approach this pleasant place. Sometimes at night cat Tosha even moved to his master's feet. And over time, the cat began to move very closer to Valery's head. Tosha felt great there, like in paradise. He purred quite loudly as he tried to sing nightly lullabies for Valery. While feeling his master head, Tosha felt so good, that he began to snore. This did not bother Valery, and even amused, creating additional warmth and comfort. They snore happily together in unison.

Despite the effort of the masters to equalize the puppy in the same rights with the cat, Tosha always felt his privileged position and took advantage of this. And the good-natured dog easily accepted and recognized his authority. Sometimes Break had hard time with the cat. But most of the time, he understood that the happy life in a small apartment is important for all. So the cat and the dog were friends, despite their incredibly contradictory characters. They disproved the proverb about the opposing sides of these creatures by their peaceful lives. And the old sentence of "living like a cat and a dog" did not sparkle with truth at all.

***

Family vacation

Once before the family trip to the south, dog Break got very sick. Every year all

necessary vaccinations were done for the dog and for the cat. But the dog was every day out playing with other dogs, and once he got a very serious canine "plague." Nobody expected this at all. Trying to save the beloved dog and cure this serious illness, the girl Lila began to give him the prescribed injections.

At that time in Russia there were no "one-time" syringes. Every four hours, Lila boiled the syringes in the kitchen, and injected the dog with medicine. This treatment was supposed to last for several months. And the family has long bought tickets to the south vacation. It was impossible to postpone this long-awaited trip to Gelendzik. So, the family collected their luggage and took a train to South.

On the train, loving his dog, Valery spent all days and nights in the vestibule with still sick Break. And Lila four times a day was continuing to give dog all necessary injections. Break understood that they were trying to help him, and courageously endured all the suffering. He dutifully and silently tolerated everything that the good girl Lila did to him. Dog's love for his master was his strongest feeling. The dog does not know love for himself.

***

Vacation

This time the whole family came to Gelendzik again to the good grandmother Anna. But this time - already with a cat and a dog. Kind grandmother gave them again the same distant room with a terrace and a separate entrance to the courtyard.

At that time all stores in Gelendzhik was quite empty, as well as throughout the country. There was enough fish for everyone on the coast of the Black Sea. Therefore, for the whole vacation, the main food for the whole family was the cheapest fish called capelin and hake.

And this time, the cat Tosha several times dared to run away for the night and useless dates. The dog got used to serving and helping everyone. Therefore, knowing that, Tosha told Break that he planned to go away for a new nightly adventure. Tosha hoped that Break would protect him, as well. But remembering the cat's tales of the past adventures with a local gang of cats, Break followed Tosha and quickly brought him back. Then still weak dog slightly scolded Tosha, reminding him of the danger of walking alone.

Instead of escorting Tosha through the challenging neighborhood, still weak from the illness, Brake loudly barked throughout the whole district. And all night he was echoed by many other local dogs. Their barks did not inferior him in the volume and bitterness. And now, in addition to the nightly yelling of the local cats, Alena, Lila and Valery could not fall asleep from the dog noise and excitements. Tosha was listening to the nightly dog's concerts on the terrace. Then, he sweetly fell asleep in the morning. He dreamed that when he would return to St. Petersburg, he could tell about his new trip to his friends. But he decided to tell about it from the top of his safe balcony. He anticipated the surprise of all the aristocrats of St. Petersburg and their enthusiasm for his southern adventures. It was especially important for Tosha that now he had a witness of his nocturnal adventures. It was his friend Break.

***

Dog School

Returning to St. Petersburg, the mistress Alena decided that their dog should fulfill its mission. He must serve and guard the apartment. Therefore, for this special training, it was decided to send Break to study at a dog school.

Tosha immediately felt that Break had received new special privilege. Tosha never wanted to stay home alone as before, and asked to take him with the dog under the supervision of the girl Lila and the artist Valera.

When they would return from the classes, Tosha scold Brake for some miscalculations and read him instructions on how and what to do next time in school. Patient Break took everything peacefully, remembering that Tosha had more experience in everyday affairs.

Finally, one spring, the artist Valery and the girl Lila put Tosha in a huge basket and took him to a dog school. There, all Shepherds stayed in a row and began to conduct their exam for the attention.

It was here that Tosha had to show that he was a real hero, and indeed could be useful. He was very glad that he could do something important for everyone and demonstrate his confidence. He was released on the walk in front of the long line of dogs. A brave cat walked slowly past the huge dogs. Tosha raised his tail as a pipe for the greater impression.

A line of shepherd dogs, including Break, was supposed to sit quietly, not expressing any reaction to their natural antipode. But still, some of them, especially emotional students, alarmingly and reservedly growled and grimaced. And others decided to just look the other way, and not to try to attack the cat. Only Break, accustomed to all sorts of Tosha's tricks, just yawned with the boredom.

After several months, Break graduated from the dog's school with the honors. Then, he began to receive the first prizes at many competitions, where the girl Lila took him to. And soon his whole dog's chest sparkled with all sorts of rewards.

Dog Break was very talented, but he was too kind to be a guard. Although he had a natural terrifying appearance, but in fact, he could not be taught or aggressive. So the master's dream of a dog guarding of the apartment was not destined to come true.

In any case, the artist Valera, mistress Alena and the girl Lila loved their pets. Break was an equal member of the family. But to everything else, he was still like a child for the artist

Valery. The main goal of the mistress Alena (to make everyone busy) was successful, and everyone was happy. But life continued to wind up its natural circles and twists.

Circumstances

Suddenly, once, out of nowhere, "perestroika" came to Russia. The different new reforms began. It was beginning of the new and unusual way of life, to which people were not accustomed. Suddenly all was rolled downhill. Many enterprises began to close, large and seemingly unshakable organizations disappeared, as if they had never been. Many people lost their jobs. A vast country that existed for seventy years, the Soviet Union disappeared

into one-part. Many people in Russia have lost themselves under the new conditions of breaking old foundations. They did not know how to live on and perceived social change with bitterness.

Mother Alena spun "like a squirrel in a wheel", working with tourists in different cities. She had to help, raise and educate her daughter Lila. Mother Alena was the one who always supported the whole family.

The artist Valery did not have a stable work, had nothing to live on. One day he left St. Petersburg forever. He took his cat Tosha with him to his motherland, to his mother's house in Ukraine. There he painted the walls of the cathedral, created icons and new paintings.

The cat Tosha lived happily for another eighteen years. Valery left his dog Break with his friends in St. Petersburg and did not give his address to mother Alena. The absolute devotion and love of the dog Break to his absent owner resulted in a strong longing and a broken heart. Soon, dog Break went to the other world.

In several years, mother Alena and her daughter Lila went overseas for a new life. And only twenty-five years later, on the Internet, they found the already famous artist Valery Bulat. Valery wrote to them about how the cat Tosha left him forever and went to the other world. Valery wrote:

"The last three months before leaving me for the other world, Tosha almost could not walk. But he tried very hard. Once, his back legs completely failed. Shortly before his final departure, he climbed under the closet. It looked like he felt something, and wanted to hide from it.

I carefully pulled him out from under the closet and laid him on the sofa. Then I lay down

next to my cat Tosha. I put my palm under his head. Tosha was breathing heavily and looked at me with very sad eyes. I spoke comforting words to him for a long time.

Suddenly, several beads of the huge bitter tears rolled from his eyes right into my palm. He did not want to leave me, and quietly said to me: "Muurr. Thank you for everything. I love you forever."

It was 10:45 pm. My good, old friend Tosha left me forever. After some sorrow, I buried him not far from my house under an old cherry tree. Every time I go to my work in the morning, I send him greetings. I remember our happy times with him in our happy apartment in St. Petersburg. I remember all magical stories of all cats of that wonderful city on the Rive Neva. But life was going on..."

***

Tosha's Dream

Once Tosha saw a strange dream. In his amazing dream, Tosha told his master, the artist Valery, where all the cats fly away from the Earth life. This dream said that all people, as well as all cats and dogs, all belong to the same moon. And Tosha described:

"It seemed that I was running in a beautiful field and smell grass: I do not remember any pain, death was like one big smell. And then it smelled of honey and mint, I flew into the grass to the whole ears. And I decided that in the new life (ninth) I will be the same who I was before, only better.

This place was called Paradise. All doors were always open here. It was cat's paradise. All cats wandered across Paradise in search of a home. And I wanted to be in the favorite warm hands, which would smell as the hands of my beloved artist.

It was the sun (looked like the sun I remember from the Earth in the window and in the South trip. It looked like a fish on the dish.

We were all here as the common cats. It is always warm, clean and dry, no rain, no snowstorm here. At night some cats dreams of dogs, growls at them in the sleep, but not too much. I am dreaming that I am running again in the field. Is everyone free to choose? I'm just a cat, I don't know anything. "

One Moon to Love

The other time, cat Tosha came out onto the roof and saw a huge moon. Also, he saw a ghost of a huge cat from another life. This huge cat roamed the rooftops with a butterfly net and enjoyed the huge moon. And strange birds flew past him, and some characters of St. Petersburg and some monuments flew by. Cat Tosha sat there for a long time. Then he decided that all this is also just a dream, which will soon pass, and again everything will happen again.

He knew now that we all live under one Moon. The only one moon was shining down on Tosha's roof, and shining on the one Earth. The Earth also belongs to only one moon.

One Moon shining for all, for animals and for people. It was important to keep the peace in the Earth. Cat Tosha thought, that it the same as to keep the good peace in the apartment where he lived..

So he wanted that all under the one Moon would be just living happy and enjoy every real day. Whatever day would bring, there will be still flowers to smell, the good fish to eat, and some kind people to love.

***

Our pets

The most popular pets for many people are cats and dogs. They are the most intelligent, easy to raise, most comfortable for living with a person.

Animals are infinitely devoted to the house, become attached to the person and love him passionately. They try to please the owner as much as they can. They do not know the

word "betrayal." In some good families, pets become family members. But it also happens that people forget that animals have their own feelings and simple thoughts. And when animals grow up, they can be thrown to the mercy of fate.

It is caring for pets bring up the best qualities in a person. And it's best to start doing this from the childhood. When a person treats animals carefully, with love and care, so most often he will relate to other people. How much time a person would give to a cat or dog, the same way he would behave in any relationship.

Cats always surprise people. If the cat gets lost, it can still overcome hundreds of kilometers, but return to its beloved home. People consider a cat as a comfort at home and protection from mice and adversities. Some say that cats reduce the risk of serious illness and even prolong life. The elders say that there are two ways to become happier and forget about adversity: music and cats. You should not be shy to caress, take pictures of your pets, and share your joy with friends. This, scientists say, strengthens the nerves and helps to survive stress. It is proved: stroking cat reduces blood pressure. They like to warm themselves and instinctively try to settle in the warmest place. The live heat of a cat very effectively soothes pain and helps fight inflammation. In honor of the some cats, people put monuments around the world.

***

About the author

The author of the trilogy is Elena Pankey. She has created many fascinating books in Russian and English. Books published in Europe and America.

Two oil paintings on canvas are down below. The first one is the portrait of Elena Pankey (Bulat) with her beloved cat Tosha. The portrait was painted in 1983 by her ex-husband, Valery Bulat. It was done in Leningrad (St. Petersburg), shortly after they got married. Some painting is stored in California in Elena's house.

The second painting is an auto portrait of the artist, Valery Bulat with his beloved dog, Break. This painting is stored in the artist's house in Zaporozhe.

The book also contains slightly modified drawings by the artist Tatyana Rodionova. Theses drawings dedicated to the cats of St. Petersburg. All photos and art slightly changed and redone by Elena Bulat. *No copyright infringement is intended.*

***
All rights reserved

The author is Elena Pankey (Bulat). All rights reserved. No part of this publication may be reproduced, reprinted, stored in a computer memory, or copied in any form or by any means, including photocopying, recording, or other electronic or mechanical methods, without the prior written permission of the publisher (Elena Pankey), unless cited in brief . The title of the book is published in the United States of America. The main category of the book is Pets. Another category is Sculpture. The first edition was done in 2020. No copyright infringement is intended. To obtain permission for any publication, write to the publisher "Caution: Permission Coordinator" at: www.TangoCaminito.com